Mischief, Mayhem and *NOT* Burning the House Down

By Jessica L. Elliott

Dear Mom and Dad

Because a paltry "To Mom and Dad" would hardly be apology/bribe enough for the contents of this book. First of all, I would like to thank you for teaching us kids to use our imaginations and to read. In a day and age when television and video games take more and more of children's time, I appreciate the fact that we were encouraged to make our own games, play outside and discover the adventure of a good book.

Second, I would like to remind you that we really did attempt to follow the rules and the house never once burned down. Some of the escapades you will read about are undoubtedly ones you have already discovered whether at the time they happened or later. Some of them may be new to you. But we did try to clean up after ourselves and surprisingly no lasting damage has ever been done to any of us…except perhaps loss of sanity.

Third, I would like to tell you how very much I love and appreciate you. I'm glad that when you did catch us in some sort of mischief, you still trusted us enough to let us try again. You taught us that having an imagination is a good thing, but that sometimes it needs reined in. You taught us that the only friends that truly last a lifetime are our family members and as a result my five closest friends are my brothers and sisters. And you taught us that you would always, always love us, no matter what.

So to you, my beloved mother and father, I dedicate this book in hopes that these memories that I have cherished will bring you laughter, smiles and the memory of good times.

Your Loving Daughter,

Jessica

Author's Note

First off, you should know that the stories in the book are based around actual events from my life. Some of them have been embellished upon and perhaps even exaggerated a little. Let's be honest. When you have a great imagination, things only get wilder and more exciting in the retelling. But they are true stories. The events that are described really happened. However, since it would take a very long time for me to describe the eighteen years of my life before going to school, I've condensed it down and events happen closer together in the book than they did in reality and not necessarily in sequential order. I've also changed the names of people who are not direct family members to protect the unfortunate victims of our mischief.

Second, I can think of only five types of people who might read this book. To each of you, I have some notes for you to consider.

1. You are an oldest child hoping to discover a way to stay out of the trouble that you or your siblings have caused. Take it from an oldest child: you will not be able to smile or reason your way out of trouble. But here's some advice; learn how to make cookies. It's a lot harder to get really mad if the house smells like fresh baked cookies. This can also be a good bribe for those younger siblings who helped you get into the trouble in the first place.

2. You are a middle/youngest child hoping to discover new and novel ways to get the oldest in your family into trouble. Please don't try the things we did; unless you are quite sure that your parents are either very understanding or very oblivious. And you should probably cut the oldest child in your family some slack. Trust me; they can get into quite enough trouble without your help. My advice, the next time you're trying

to pin something on that older sibling, consider fessing up. Like I said, the oldest can get into enough trouble on their own.

3. You are an only child wondering what it's like to have siblings. These stories will cause one of two reactions. You'll either thank your parents for being the only child or you will feel very left out. I hope that you will not feel left out. Perhaps you also have a vivid imagination and have been able to discover the joy of make-believe. In which case, you've probably been able to get yourself into as much trouble as we did. I applaud your creativity! I hope that you will sit back with this book and enjoy the adventure.

4. You are a parent wanting to know what your children do while you're away. CLOSE THIS BOOK AND RUN FAR AWAY FROM IT!!! The truth is my siblings and I have way too much imagination to be kept in one house. Your kids are probably much milder and if they're not, you don't want to know everything that goes on while you're away. Children with imagination can always be trusted to discover some sort of mischief while you're gone. And the more imagination they have, the messier that mischief will get. My advice to you is to pick this book up after your kids are grown. Then you probably won't mind so much what happened while you were gone. And if you don't mind now, then read on and enjoy!

5. You are in an airport with a long layover and this was the most promising title you came across. To you I give my sincere apologies. There is very little seriousness or intellect to be found within the pages of this novel. But perhaps like me, you enjoy a little mind candy to get you through a long wait. If that is indeed the case, sit back, try to relax on that horridly uncomfortable chair and enjoy the fun.

Table of Contents

The Rules

Mom had very few rules for us when she left the house. In fact, she only had three:

1. Do not kill or permanently maim each other.

2. When you make a mess, clean it up before I get home.

3. Do not burn the house down.

Now, these seem like very simple rules. But as has been stated, each of us children was blessed (or cursed) with a vivid imagination. Try as we might the rules sometimes got, well, bent a little bit. Okay, maybe they got bent a lot a bit. Oh, alright, sometimes the rules were downright broken. But, I'm happy to say that in all the mischief that my siblings and I got ourselves into, not once did we burn the house down. That was the one rule that never got bent, tweaked or broken. The other two are a whole other story.

Misadventure Begins

Just before I was allowed to watch the kids myself, Mom and Dad went down to Dallas so that they could do work in the LDS temple there. A babysitter had been called to stay overnight and watch us until they returned sometime in the evening of the second day. She was recently engaged and so had spent much of the evening too excited to get much sleep. By mid-afternoon of the second day, she had us put in a quiet movie with the intention of everyone taking a siesta, as she put it. "Go get your favorite blankets and pillows so you guys can be comfortable," she said. "Bekah, since Jessica picked the movie last night, it's your turn to pick a movie to watch."

Bekah ran downstairs to pick a movie and the rest of us gathered our blankets and pillows. I was even nice enough to grab Bekah's for her since she was busy picking a movie. Soon we had all gathered up again and

Bekah popped *The Secret Garden* into the VHS player. James rolled his eyes at her. "Again?"

"Hey, Allison said I could pick." Bekah said stubbornly.

"Alright, no fighting," Allison warned.

The argument ceased and everyone made little nests on the ground. We could tell she was tired and we weren't about to tell her that we all knew "siesta" was a grown-up way of saying nap. Most of us hadn't taken a nap in several years and had no intention of actually going to sleep. But since she was giving us free rein to make a mess of the living room, we took full advantage of it. Soon there were blankets and pillows strewn about the floor and we were watching the movie. Bekah and I both loved *The Secret Garden*, especially the scene in the garden when they're taking photographs. Our favorite part was the garden swing hanging from the tall tree in the garden.

"Hey, Jessica," Bekah whispered (Allison had fallen asleep and we didn't want to wake her), "wouldn't it be cool if we had a garden swing?"

"It would, but we don't have a garden."

"There's the tree in the front yard that we climb in. We could put a swing there." Bekah was usually the instigator of our mischief and if not her, it was me and she took charge of it.

"That wouldn't work. The fence is too close. Besides, we don't have any wood to make a swing seat from."

Bekah paused to think. "Well, what if we built the swing inside?"

At this point, James was listening in. "That would be awesome!" he said, a little too loudly.

"Shhh!"

We all turned to the couch where Allison was still sound asleep. After a moment, we all turned to each other again. Now everyone was in on the secret. "How would we do that?" I asked her.

"We could use the railing upstairs and hang it over the stairs going to our room," she pointed out.

I glanced again at Allison. She was really, really tired. If we were quiet, she would sleep through the whole episode and never know that anything had happened. "Alright. Eliza, go get a piece of long rope from Daddy's Scout box. Bekah, you and I will tie it to the railing."

Eliza scampered off to the rope box and brought the longest rope Dad had. Soon Bekah and I were tying the ends to the upstairs railing. Then we all went back downstairs. "My idea, so I get first swing," Bekah said.

Everyone shrugged. It wasn't worth an argument. After she had a turn, everyone else tried. When James got off the swing he frowned. "The rope hurts my bottom."

"Yeah, it does a bit. Maybe we could use a pillow as a seat." I grabbed my pillow and tried to put it onto the ropes.

Steven took his turn and fell off. "Ouch."

"Well, that didn't work," Bekah scoffed.

"Have any better ideas?" I retorted.

"What if we made a vine swing like in *Swiss Family Robinson*?" Eliza asked before the fight could really get going.

"But we don't have water to land on like they did. We would crash through the girls' room door and hurt ourselves."

"Not if we opened our door," Bekah said.

"And we could pile all the blankets and pillows at the bottom of the stairs and into the room for a soft landing," James pointed out.

I knew I should have told them that the fun was over, but in truth I'd always wanted to try out a vine swing. "Alright, but this rope is too long. Go get a shorter one."

Eliza went to get the rope and the rest of us quietly got our blankets and pillows out of the living room. Soon there were blankets sprawled across the landing and spilling into the girls' room. Pillows were strewn about on top to cushion us as we swung. James was allowed the first swing and we took turns for a while. It was going along great until James' last turn. He filled his lungs with air and just as he started to swing, let out a Tarzan yell to wake the dead. Okay, maybe not the dead; but it did wake Allison.

Bolting upright on the couch, she yelped, "What happened?" Her eyes adjusted and she saw the rope dangling from the upstairs railing. "What is that?"

"A sing," Steven announced. "You wanna tun?"

"No I don't want a turn!" Allison replied, getting up from the couch and placing her hands on her hips. "What were you thinking? You could have gotten hurt or broken something. Your parents will be here any minute and if they catch you with that mess there's going to be trouble."

"You won't tell them, will you?" James asked, putting on his best pleading face.

Allison looked at each of us. Five pairs of big eyes looked back at her. "If you get it cleaned up in the next two minutes, then I won't tell your parents what you were up to. But only if it's all cleaned up."

The five of us kids scrambled to pick everything up and get it put away properly. I untied the rope from the railing and put it away in the Scout box while the others grabbed armfuls of pillows and blankets from the landing downstairs. The chaos caused a few little scuffles.

"That's my blanket!"

"Who cares? I'm putting it away."

"But it's mine."

"Stop fighting and clean it up," Allison warned. "Only one minute left."

"Ouch, you stepped on me."

"Well, I'm trying to hurry."

"Has anyone seen my pillow?"

"I un-gee."

"Thirty seconds," Allison called.

"Who has my throw?"

"It's probably in the pile upstairs."

"That's not put away."

"Ten seconds."

"I un-gee."

Allison continued counting down the seconds until she'd reached zero. At that point five out of breath children smiled up at her. The landing was cleaner then than it had been before the would-be garden swing. She smiled. "Alright, it's our secret. Don't do it again."

Steven pulled on her pant leg. "I un-gee," he said more insistently.

"Well then let's make dinner," Allison replied. "Come help me in the kitchen, Jessica. The rest of you put in a movie and this time watch it sitting on the couch. I'll be watching you," she added, eying each of us. "Eliza, it's your turn to pick."

As Eliza put in *Swiss Family Robinson*, Allison and I worked on making spaghetti for dinner. It wasn't long after that my parents arrived. They were greeted by a barrage of voices welcoming them home.

"How were they?" Mom asked as she came into the kitchen.

"They were great," Allison said. "Didn't have any problems at all."

The rest of us shared a conspiratorial smile. Allison had been true to her word. But if we had thought about it logically, it wasn't in her best interest to tell anyway. Admitting to falling asleep on the job when watching five rambunctious kids wouldn't have done her any favors.

Bank in a Wall

It would be dishonest of me to say that we never rebuilt the swing, but the next time we did it was when I was the babysitter. And that wasn't the only thing we were guilty of building. Bekah and I were expert safe-builders. Mom and Dad had always encouraged us to use our imaginations and be creative. Unfortunately we were sometimes more destructive with our creativity than either of them wanted. When our family lived in the base housing at McConnell AFB, we decided that we needed to have a safe in our room having just watched *No Deposit, No Return.* But we didn't have a safe in our room or anywhere in the house. So we decided to build one and I'm sure you can guess what happened then. That's right, we knocked a small hole in the wall that was just big enough for us to stick our hands in and drop toys down. And our arms were skinny and limber enough that we could reach down and pick them up again. Now when we lived on base, they had maintenance people who would come and fix things when they were broken. So when Mom and Dad found out about our "safe", they called the repair guy and he came and patched up the wall. Hopefully we got all the toys out first; otherwise there might still be some old Duplos shoved into those walls.

After we moved to the house that we spent most of our childhood in, we had all but forgotten about safe-building; until Mom put in *No Deposit, No Return* for us to watch one afternoon while she ran a few errands. Bekah looked at me mischievously. "We should build a new safe in the boys' room," she said.

"I don't know if my arms are small enough anymore," I replied.

"Mine are. You can put stuff in and if you can't get to it, I'll pull it out for you."

"What are we doing?" Eliza asked.

"We're going to build a safe," Bekah said and up the stairs she marched, the rest of us tagging along behind. "We're going to need something to start the hole with," she stated.

"What if we hit the wall with a brick?" James asked, holding up one of the Duplo blocks.

"That might work," Bekah mused. She took the block from him and started hitting the wall. At first, it just made dents in the wall. "Jessica, I can't quite do it. You try."

I know I should have said no. But instead I said, "Okay." I took the brick and hit the wall a little more forcefully than Bekah had. It scratched up the wall, but didn't really put a hole in it. "I don't think this is going to work. How did we do it at the other house?"

"Oh yeah, we used the doorknob!" Bekah took over again. She pulled the door almost closed and then slammed it into the wall. Then she started scraping at the hole with her fingers, breaking off chunks of dry wall and scattering them on the floor.

"Don't make too much of a mess," I warned. "Mom will see it."

"Well, the little kids can pick it up," Bekah replied. Eliza and James dutifully set about collecting bits of wall as it fell until Bekah declared that it was finished. There was now a hole about the size of a large grapefruit in the wall. "There. Now we just need some toys to keep safe."

"How about the giraffe?" James offered, handing her the little Duplo animal.

"Good idea."

We gathered more toys and I asked, "What are we going to use to cover the hole? The safe in the movie had a door."

Bekah thought for a moment. "We'll use the bedroom door. The hole is right where the doorknob is, so that will keep the safe hidden from Mom and Dad."

It worked, for a while, and the hole got gradually larger until it was the size of a small cantaloupe. Then one day Mom and Dad found our secret safe.

"What is this?" Mom demanded after gathering us all in the room.

Five children hung their heads. Bekah replied, "It's a safe."

"I thought you girls had outgrown that," Dad said. We could hear the disappointment in his tone.

"How do you know it was us?" Bekah demanded.

Dad gave her a look and she fell quiet again.

"They have safes in the movies. It seemed like a good idea," I said, hoping that would give us a little leeway.

"They have *real* safes in movies. They don't just knock holes in the walls and call it a safe," Mom pointed out. "What were you planning on doing with it?"

"It keeps our animals safe," James said.

"How do you plan on getting it fixed?" Mom asked.

"You can just call the guy to fix it again," I said, remembering the maintenance crew from the base.

Dad decided to put an end to our safe building days the best way he knew how. "You are the repairmen. You are all going to help fix this hole. And you are going to do it the hard way."

"You're also going to have to help paint that part of the wall. In the colors I want," Mom added when gleeful glints entered our eyes.

For the rest of the day, we worked on fixing the hole in the wall. We had to go with him to the lumber store to buy the materials. There was no laughing and chatting during this trip like in most shopping trips. When we got to the check out, the cashier asked, "What project are we working on today?"

"They're learning to patch walls," Dad replied.

The saleslady stifled a laugh. "Kick a hole in the wall?"

"Not exactly," we replied.

"We bit a say," Steven said.

"What?" she asked.

"We built a safe," I translated. Steven had a severe speech impediment and often had difficulty being understood by people outside our family. The rest of us were used to translating for him when we went out. Most of the time, however, he only spoke to us.

Dad took us back home and then we had to cut, with his supervision, the piece of dry wall to replace what we had knocked out. Then we had to put the mudding in, scrape it, and put the special pieces of tape in. And he made sure that it was not a fun fix. We had to work hard and it had to be perfect. There was no smiling, no laughter, and really not a lot of talking either while we worked. When we were finally finished, Dad asked, "Are you going to be building any more safes in the walls?"

"No, Daddy," we said in unison.

"Good."

"Do we get to paint today?" James asked hopefully.

"No, this has to dry completely first. You'll be painting tomorrow," Dad replied.

When we went to bed that night Bekah and I agreed that perhaps it would be better to get a real safe instead of building one. "But," she admitted as we were falling asleep, "that was a lot of fun."

"It was while it lasted," I agreed.

It's Not My Fault…Exactly

It's always been the family joke that because I'm the oldest everything is my fault. Sometimes it didn't feel like a joke. If something went wrong I was often the first one blamed whether or not I was actually responsible for whatever mischief had ensued. Now to be fair, it also depended on what had happened. Bekah was the best at destroying, and then attempting to put back together, various items in the house. She could take apart the doorknobs, though she had trouble putting them back the way they were. And there were more unwanted McDonalds toys that underwent "surgery" in our house than probably anywhere else in the world. . So usually if something was taken apart I didn't get in trouble for it.

But if there was any type of injury or mess involved, I'd hear about it. And that tended to happen a lot. Unfortunately, I was good at teaching my siblings various tricks that seem great and fun…until someone gets hurt. In a real oxy-moron, I have a very good sense of balance, despite being incredibly clumsy. I quickly learned that if I put my hands and feet flush against the sides of a doorway and then, one at a time, moved them up I could "walk" up the doorway and then balance myself at the top. I could stay there for several minutes before my hands and feet got too sweaty and I started to slip down. I taught Bekah and Eliza how to do this and then it became a game. Who could stay up top the longest? I always won and this game in and of itself was fairly harmless. The doorway into the kitchen was a standard doorway, so even if you fell down, it didn't hurt you too badly because you weren't that high up. But then the game evolved further and the person on top became a bridge for the others to run under until their arms and legs gave way. And that's when someone got hurt. Eliza was at the top, pushing her hands and feet against the sides of the doorway, trying not to slip. She never lasted long up there. Just as Bekah was running underneath Eliza's legs, her hands slipped and she crashed down on top of Bekah's head. There was all sorts of ruckus between the two bodies hitting the floor, Bekah and Eliza both starting to wail and various items that had been on the island falling to the floor. Soon I realized that there was blood involved and before I had the chance to get them, Mom and Dad came barreling down the stairs from their room.

"What happened?" Mom demanded while Dad scooped Bekah up.

"They were climbing on the doorway," I said, "and Eliza fell."

"Jessica Lyn Schofield, how many times have I told you not to do that?"

"But I wasn't doing it," I argued. And this time I wasn't. I was just watching.

"Amy, I need a washcloth now! We have to stop the bleeding." Dad called.

"You get your father a washcloth now. You better hope they aren't hurt too badly," Mom scolded.

I pouted and got the washcloth like I was told. When I got downstairs where Dad was trying to comfort Bekah, there was blood everywhere. I handed him the washcloth and sat down heavily. I don't do well with the sight of blood. Mom called the doctor's office and explained briefly what had happened. Soon Mom, Dad and Bekah were heading to the clinic while Eliza, James and I were to sit on the couch and not move. James looked at me. "What did we do?"

"We didn't do anything," I told him. "Eliza and Bekah were playing a game and they fell down."

"Then why is Mommy mad at you?" he asked.

"I don't know." Actually, I knew exactly why Mom and Dad were mad at me. It was because I was the oldest and that meant that everything was my fault. This didn't improve my temper any and I sat pouting.

Before too long, they had returned. Bekah's nose was broken and there was nothing that could be done for it. I was given a very long lecture about setting a good example.

"But I didn't do anything," I insisted, sulking at the fact that I was the one getting in trouble. Not Eliza for falling on Bekah. Not Bekah for playing along. I was in trouble.

"Who taught them how to climb the doorway?" Dad asked.

"I did."

"Would they have done it if you hadn't taught them?"

While I was thinking that they probably would have figured it out since it's not that hard to do, I did know better than to talk back to my parents when they were mad. "No," I said meekly.

"So you need to set a good example for your brother and sisters. They watch what you do and want to be like you," Mom said.

Sitting Arrangements

Mom and Dad were very laid-back about how we sat at dinner, for the most part. But when they couldn't stand the arguing anymore, they did make certain rules. When we were little Bekah thought she was the only one worthy of having the red plastic cup. Mom has talked with other moms and they all agreed that whoever thought it was a good idea to have two of each color except red in the set of cups was a moron. The red cup became the most highly sought after cup at dinnertime because there was only one. No one wanted the yellow, the green or the blue because there were two of those ones. Anyone could have one of those colors. But the red cup was special. And so it was while we were young that Mom had a rotating schedule for the red cup going in age order from the oldest to the youngest. As we got older, the plastic cups were only for the littlest kids and soon

Bekah and I didn't have the opportunity to fight over who got the red cup. We were big enough to use glasses.

Unfortunately, Bekah also had this idea that she was the only one who could sit by Dad at dinnertime. It caused some minor scuffles and arguments when we were young, but for the most part that's all there was. When Steven started sitting at the table without the high chair, suddenly the fact that Bekah always sat by Dad became a major issue. The rest of us had gotten over arguing with Bekah over who got to sit there, but Steven wasn't going to give up so easily. And seeing him get riled up about it reminded the rest of us of the vast unfairness of our dinnertime seating.

Now usually we didn't plot against each other, but every now and again something would come up that would cause several, if not all, of the opposing siblings to rally against the unlucky one. Bekah was the unlucky one this time and she was in for a nasty surprise. All of us were in it together. The plotting party began in the boys' room while Bekah was doing something else. I'm not even sure I remember what it was anymore. Maybe it was her turn to help with dinner.

In any case, the four of us sat in the boys' room together planning our revenge. "She ah-way get to sit dere," Steven complained. "I wanna sit by Daddy too."

"Maybe we could put sitting cards on everyone's plate," Eliza suggested. "It's my turn to set the table. I could put a card with people's names on them and they have to sit there."

"I've tried that before," I pointed out. "Bekah just moved the card to the spot next to Dad and put my name at the opposite end of the table."

James was looking mischievous. "I have a better idea," he said with an evil grin. "We could tie her up."

"What? How are we going to tie her up?" I asked. "You don't really think Dad's going to just let us use his ropes for Scouts, do you?"

"He didn't find out when we used them for the swings," James argued. "Besides, we wouldn't need rope. Mom hasn't emptied the sock basket in a long time. There's tons of socks we could use." Mom had a small, square basket that she used to keep the mismatched socks in. I'm pretty sure that most of those socks were either eaten by the dryer (admit it, you still believe there's a sock-eating monster in your dryer), accidently lost in people's rooms or were lost on purpose. The ugliest socks tended to stay in the basket the longest. And when a few months had gone by and Mom was sure that she had washed every single sock in the house, she would empty the sock basket, mate as many socks as she could and then throw out any socks that were still single.

"You mean tie her up with socks?" I asked.

"Yeah," James said. "It would be fun. I just learned how to tie knots in Cub Scouts. We could tie them really, really tight and then we all get to sit down at the dinner table before she does. Then one of us will get to sit by Dad."

"I wan fur tun," Steven added.

"Okay, Steven gets the first turn," I agreed. "How are we going to catch her? She's really fast."

"Not if all four of us are working together. She can't get away if it's all of us," Eliza pointed out.

"Besides, if Jessica sits on her, she'll never be able to get away," James threw in.

"Hey!" I said indignantly. Sometimes being the oldest and biggest has some disadvantages. The younger ones think you're huge.

"What? You are bigger than her. If you sit on her back, she won't be able to get away from us."

And so it began. I'm ashamed to admit that all of us, even Steven, knew that what we were doing was totally wrong and would get us into huge trouble once Mom found out. But at that point, we were committed and a Schofield never backs out of a commitment. Mom told me that she needed to run to the store for some last-minute groceries. "Watch over everyone please. And don't get into trouble."

Sorry, Mom, I thought while saying, "Alright."

Mom left and we found Bekah sitting on the couch reading a book. Eliza had positioned herself next to the sock basket and what ensued next was a dog pile of such epic proportions that professional wrestling couldn't have done better. The boys tackled Bekah to the floor, her book flying across the room. Bekah started shouting and trying to get away and I did my job. I sat square in the middle of her back.

"Jessica, I can't breathe!" she squealed. "Get off of me."

"I'm not that fat," I said and stayed in place as best I could. She is pretty good at wriggling away, but with all four of us working against her, she didn't stand a chance. James somehow managed not to get kicked in the face as Bekah struggled to get free and he managed to tie her legs together. Eliza was getting clawed while trying to tie Bekah's hands together. Then we turned her over as she continued to yell at us.

"What are you doing? Stop it!" she screamed.

"No, it ow tun," Steven announced.

Bekah wriggled some more as I tied a sock between her hands and her feet so she couldn't get away. If you're imagining a roped calf, that's pretty much what she looked like. Soon she was hogtied and could scarcely move. James was in the process of trying to gag her when Mom and Dad both walked into the house. Dad had just happened to get home from work at the same time Mom got back from the store.

"What on earth are you doing?" she demanded.

Dad was starting to swell up like a bullfrog and I knew instantly that maybe hogtying Bekah had been a big mistake. Okay, maybe it was a huge mistake. Alright, alright, it was downright wrong. Dad made us all sit down, cross-legged with our arms folded, while he untied Bekah. She glared at all of us as Dad asked, "Who started it?"

"They all did it," Bekah replied angrily. Her arms and legs had bright red marks from the socks chafing against her skin. Hot, angry tears spilled down her cheeks and she looked at each of us with utmost hatred.

"Jessica, tell me what happened," Mom said. Her tone indicated that any trying to butter her up would work about as well as using cactus needles to make a comfortable pillow.

"Well, we were all tired of Bekah always getting to sit by Dad and so we were trying to make her sit somewhere else tonight. We thought that if she was tied up when we were sitting down, then one of us could get to sit by Dad."

"You could have asked her to sit somewhere else," Dad replied sternly.

"But we've tried asking and she always says no," James argued.

Mom put a hand on Dad's arm before he could say anything else. "Bekah, do you let the others sit by Dad?"

"That's my spot," Bekah sniffed. "They can sit anywhere else at the table."

"Bekah, it's not fair if you always get to sit by Dad. The other children want to have turns too," Mom replied. Then she turned to the rest of us. "But, even if it's not fair, what you did was wrong."

"Look at your sister," Dad interrupted. "Look at her arms."

We turned ashamed faces towards Bekah. There were swollen parts on her wrists and ankles and a few places had been rubbed raw and were bleeding a little.

"You did that to her. Is that what Jesus would have done?" Dad demanded.

"No."

"Then why did you do it?"

At this point there wasn't a dry eye in the room. "I wan a tun to sit by you," Steven whimpered.

"Well, tonight only Mom can sit by me. The rest of you will be sitting on the couch in the living room," Dad said. "And starting tomorrow there will be seating assignments for every meal that I'm home for. Of all the ridiculous things to fight over! Sitting next to me at dinner doesn't mean that I love you any more or any less than I love the person sitting next to you. You never fight over who gets to sit by Mom."

"We always get to sit by Mom," Eliza pointed out.

"That's beside the point," Mom said. "You children hurt one of your siblings over something petty and insignificant. I'm disappointed in you."

Those are the worst words a mother can say. If we weren't already crying, everyone was then. We sniffled and apologized to Mom and Dad and then to Bekah. Mom finished dinner and Dad went upstairs to change out of his work clothes. The rest of us sat on the couch waiting for Mom to say dinner was ready. When it was, we filed into the kitchen and folded our arms while Dad said the blessing on the food.

"Can we wat a moo-wie wi dinna?" Steven asked hopefully as he took his plate.

"No, you kids are in trouble," Mom said. "There will be no movie with dinner or afterwards."

"What if we promise to never do it again?" James added.

"No," Mom replied. "There will be no movies tonight."

We knew there was no sense attempting to change her mind, so we silently filed back into the living room with our plates and sat on the couch, using the small coffee table to hold our plates. It was perhaps the quietest meal we had ever eaten together. There was no laughter, no light-hearted chatter. Just the sounds of forks scraping plates. Once our dinners were done, Mom had me help her with the dishes while the rest went to their rooms. "I can't believe you participated in that," Mom said as she was washing. "What were you thinking?"

"I wasn't," I said. I knew it wouldn't help to start the argument over again. At this point, I knew that we hadn't really thought out what we were doing.

"You're the oldest, Jessica, you need to set a better example for your younger siblings. They look up to you."

I rolled my eyes when she couldn't see me. I was tired of having to be the example. Why couldn't someone else be the example for a change? "Okay," I said.

"I mean it, Jessica," Mom added warningly.

"I know."

For the next several months we were given a seating arrangement at dinnertime. There was no arguing over who got to sit where because there was no choice in the matter. And if someone did try to argue, they were sent to have their supper in their room and they missed out on any family activities we did that night. I suppose if we had been smart, we would have told Mom and Dad our complaint and then the seating arrangement could have been done without the hogtying experience. But then again, kids do sometimes have to learn things the hard way. And it seemed growing up that we often chose the hard way.

Don't Try This at Home

That whole message at the beginning of a lot of science movies and things like that, the one that says, "Kids, don't try this at home," was written specifically for kids like us. Only the problem is, not every movie comes with that warning. In fact most of them don't. And that's where most of our really creative ideas came from. *Candleshoe* didn't have that warning and so when the kids slid across the highly polished wood floors, we wanted to do it too. Now at first we were deterred by the fact that weren't any wood floors in our parents' house. But our kitchen did have linoleum. "That's almost like wood floors isn't it?" Bekah asked.

"Close enough," I said. "But we should probably wait until Mom isn't here. I don't think she'd like us trying to slide across the floors." As though she had heard our wish, Mom soon announced that she was going to go run some errands and would be back in a couple of hours. "Jessica, you're in charge. I want you to take care of the younger kids okay?"

"Okay Mom," I said. It was the first time she was leaving us without a babysitter for an extended period of time.

As soon as she had left, Bekah turned to me. "So, how do we slide across the floors?"

"They said they waxed the floors in the movie. Do we have any wax?" I asked.

We started looking for wax. James offered ear wax. "James, even your ears don't make that much wax," Eliza said.

"What if we all gave some?"

"That wouldn't give us nearly enough for the whole floor. Besides, that's gross." I said.

"Maybe we could use water instead of wax," Eliza suggested.

So we got out Dad's squirt bottle that he used when he was ironing clothes. We squirted down the whole floor, refilling the bottle a couple of times before putting it away again. "It makes the floor slippery,"

Bekah observed, trying to slide. "But my feet keep sticking to the floor where there isn't water. This isn't going to work."

We started searching again and soon Bekah's eyes fell on the counter where Mom had gotten out the ingredients to make cookies. "Hey, what if we used shortening?" she asked.

"That would work. It's really slick and would stick to the floor better than water," I said.

Getting out paper towels, the five of us started scooping piles of shortening onto the floor and scrubbed it in until the floor was glossy and goopy with it. "I get to try first," Bekah announced. She stepped onto the floor and slid from one end of the kitchen to the other. "It worked!" she exclaimed. Soon all of us were sliding merrily across the floor, sometimes landing on our behinds as we fell down.

Then I looked at the clock. "Mom will be home soon!" I panicked. "We better get this cleaned up or she's going to be really mad at us."

"She already will be," Eliza announced. "We used up all the shortening."

"Well, maybe she'll think she'd already finished the can," I said hopefully. "After all, sometimes she says Dad forgets to throw the can away when he finishes it off and he made cookies last. Come on, let's clean this up."

"But the water isn't doing anything," Bekah said as she picked up a rag she'd been using to try to clean the floor.

"We need to use soap," I said.

"Okay," James replied. He grabbed the bottle and started dumping dish soap on the floor.

"Don't use it all!" I cried. "Mom won't believe us if we say that Dad used up two things."

"Oh, right," he said. Soon we were all on our hands and knees scrubbing the floor. Mom got home just as we were finishing and rinsing off our rags.

"How nice of you to think of cleaning the floor for me," she said as she walked in carrying grocery sacks. "Can a couple of you help me put the groceries away?"

"Yes, Mom," we said.

When she went to make the cookies and realized that she was out of shortening, she just sighed, "Samuel." She threw the can away and asked me to go downstairs and see if we had another can in the food storage closet.

"Sure, Mom," I said. Crisis averted. Mom hadn't figured out what we had been up to and she never found out that Dad wasn't the one who emptied the shortening. She must not have asked him about it, because I'm sure he would have told her that there had been shortening left the last time he made cookies. In fact, there had been a pretty good amount of shortening left in the can when he last made cookies. But we didn't get in trouble and Mom didn't find out what we had been doing. In fact, she had praised us for being thoughtful enough to clean the floor for her. I don't think the floor had ever received such an odd treatment before, but it maintained a subtle sheen for a while after that.

The other place we gathered a lot of ideas was school. When I was in kindergarten, the art teacher taught us about an amazing artist named Michaelangelo. He was famous for painting the ceiling of the Sistine Chapel.

"How did he do it?" one of the kids asked.

"He lay on his back on a scaffold," the teacher replied. "After he finished, it's said that he could never read properly again without lying back with it."

"Wow."

"Neat!"

I love art and always have. That sparked a new idea for me to try at home. As soon as I got back, Mom asked how my day had gone and then she was busy doing something in the kitchen. Probably making dinner. I grabbed my crayons from my room and lay down on my bed. "Hmm, I can't reach the ceiling. But maybe I can reach the bottom of the table." I started to go to the dining room but was stopped by Bekah.

"Whatcha doin'?"

"Shhhh. I'm going to be Michaelangelo."

"The turtle?"

"No, the artist. He's way cooler than the turtle."

"Oh. What did he do?"

"He painted a ceiling in a chapel."

Bekah gasped. "And he didn't get in trouble for it?"

"No, they asked him to do it. Isn't that nifty?"

"Yeah. Are you going to color the ceiling?" Bekah's eyes got bigger with each word.

"No, I can't reach the ceiling. I tried. So I'm going to lie down under the table."

"Oh no you won't, I'll tell Mommy."

"No one sees the bottom of the table," I argued.

"I'm telling unless I get to color too."

"Okay we can both be Michaelangelo."

Soon we were both under the table coloring. It didn't take long for Eliza to toddle over to see what we were doing. We knew the only way to keep it to ourselves was to let her join in. We both held fingers to our lips while handing her a crayon.

"Mommy mad?" she asked.

"Nah, she'll never know. No one looks at the bottom of the table," Bekah said.

"Okay."

The three of us were soon creating masterpieces on the underside of the table. We heard Mom moving towards the dining room and quickly hid the evidence of our escapade. The table became a favorite spot for secret coloring. Many of us practiced our letters and numbers under there. We even wrote notes to each other. One time when Bekah got irritated with me, she wrote, "I am stoopid. Sined Jessica." Once I found the note I erased it as best I could. For one it was misspelled and for another I didn't want future generations thinking their aunt Jessica was stupid. But the years passed and more of us added to the table. As far as I know, Mom and Dad didn't find out about it until we moved and they were lifting the table. By then it had been so long since we had started coloring under there that there was only one thing for them to do. They both laughed. "Well, at least it was the underside and not the top."

Pinning the Blame on Dad

Dad was often the unfortunate victim of our mischievousness. Not because we would do anything to him, but rather because we found creative ways of blaming him for our misdeeds. Such as using his forgetful nature to our advantage when we emptied the shortening on the floor. But often it involved something being broken during football season. We're a competitive group, which is why when we played board games and card games as a family we never kept score. Mom and Dad wanted to prevent us from being competitive against each other. But, being competitive in sports and rooting wildly for our favorite team was perfectly acceptable and, in fact, encouraged. Dad is perhaps the most competitive of us all and during football season he can go from being the very calm, laid-back man that we know and love to a raging volcano. Now, I'm really not proud of the fact that we got Dad into trouble. And I'm even less proud of the fact that never once did we step in and say, "No, Mom, Dad didn't do it. We did." Our parents had taught us to be truthful and to take responsibility for our actions. And I'd like to think that usually we were pretty good about owning up to our misdeeds when we got caught. But if the opportunity arose for someone else to take the fall, I'm afraid we let them.

Usually the things we did weren't noticeable for some time. Mom probably wouldn't have noticed that the shortening was out the same day we "waxed" the floor if she hadn't happened to have planned on making cookies that afternoon. They didn't find out about the underside of the table being colored on for a long time because, let's face it, you never go underneath your table. And even if you do, it's to pick something up off the floor. You don't ever look up at the underside to make sure that your kids haven't been coloring up there.

Sometimes, though, the things that we did were painfully obvious. And then it took some creativity to make sure that Mom and Dad didn't notice. One particular misdeed happened the day before the Sugar

Bowl. Dad had done all of his ironing and had left the ironing board up because he was in rush to get to work, or go somewhere. I don't remember precisely why the ironing board had been left up. I do, however, remember that I was supposed to take it down and put it away.

Mom and Dad were out on a date and the rest of us were playing at home. I'm not sure how the fight started, or why. But it was during a stage when Bekah and I couldn't get along for love or money. We were constantly bickering and picking at each other. I think the biggest problem we faced was me. I was going through puberty, which is rough enough for anyone, but it made me temperamental and highly emotional. Bekah swears to this day that you could tell me to cry and I would do it, that's how easily tears came to my eyes. Dad was often convinced that I hated him because he would come home from work and have a funny look on his face and I'd start crying. It's rather embarrassing to admit that my teen years were spent trying to be a watering can; but I blame my parents. After all, they're the ones who stuck me with the name meaning, "wealthy waterfall". They should have known what they were getting themselves into. (By the way, Mom and Dad, I do love my name, even if it did curse me to be a waterfall.)

However, back to the story, Bekah and I were arguing, again, and it was growing worse and worse by the second. James, Steven and Eliza had wisely hidden in the boys' room to avoid getting pulled into it. They weren't about to get into trouble for whatever Bekah and I ended up doing to each other. We were in the living room where the ironing board still stood, the iron sitting on top of it with the cord wrapped up. The fight reached its peak when I totally lost it and shoved Bekah into the ironing board. The iron went flying into the air and Bekah and the ironing board crashed to the floor with the iron hitting Bekah's leg not long after.

For a moment all was silent and then I burst into tears. "B-Bekah, I'm s-so so-so-sorry," I sobbed. "I d-didn't m-m-mean to."

Bekah stared at me, silent tears rolling down her cheeks and then to my surprise she started to laugh.

"It's not funny!" I shouted, still sobbing.

"Yes it is," she sobbed back.

Soon both of us were laughing maniacally and bawling our eyes out. Had Mom and Dad arrived home at that moment, they probably would have taken us straight to a psych ward! Eliza poked her head out the boys' room door. "Are you two feeling better?"

"Leave us alone!" we yelled.

She ducked back into the boys' room, but not before I heard her say, "They must not be better yet."

I helped Bekah to her feet and checked the bruise she had from the iron landing on top of her. It wasn't too horribly bad and hadn't bled at all, which was good. If there was blood involved, it wouldn't matter how well we cleaned up afterwards, Mom would find out. I think she may have been part bloodhound, because anytime blood was involved in a misadventure, she would find out and ask, "What happened?" But this time we were fortunate; no blood. Then we picked up the ironing board.

"Jessica, I think we broke it," Bekah said as she lifted it up. One of the legs had bent slightly and there was a crack running down the middle of the board.

"Oh no! How are we going to hide that from Mom and Dad? I was supposed to put this away!"

"We'll just fold it up and set it against the closet door," Bekah replied. "We haven't cleaned out the closet yet anyway, so there's no room for it in there. If we put it so that the covered part of the board is facing out, then they won't see the crack in it."

"Good idea!" I said. We put the board up and then looked at it for a while. "They won't be able to tell looking at it right now. But when Dad goes to iron again, they're going to find out."

"By then maybe something else will happen to it and they won't know that it was us."

"Yeah right. What could possibly happen to the ironing board to break it worse?"

"I don't know, but Mom's been saying they needed a new one anyway," Bekah retorted.

A second argument was prevented by Steven coming down the stairs. "Je-ee-ja. I un-gee."

"Is it time to make dinner?" I asked him with a smile. Steven could always diffuse any situation with his bright blue eyes and cute, dimpled smile.

"Uh-huh."

"Okay, let's make dinner." I scooped him up and put him on the counter while I made up spaghetti for dinner. I asked Bekah to help get out the ingredients for making the sauce and soon we had all but forgotten about the broken ironing board.

The next day we were all sitting in the living room watching the Sugar Bowl. Kansas State University was playing against Brigham Young University and it was a bloodbath. Dad was getting more and more riled as bad calls were made and poor sportsmanship reared its ugly head. He was shouting at the referees, pacing the living room and muttering. We could tell that if something didn't happen soon to make him feel better, he was going to explode. Mom kept trying to calm him down. "Honey, it's just a game," she said gently, though there was a warning note in her voice too.

"I know that, Amy," Dad snapped, though for a while he did calm down a little.

And then it happened. The ref called something on BYU and Dad lost it. "WHAT KIND OF CALL WAS THAT?!?" he bellowed and drove his fist into the ironing board which was still leaning against the closet door. The board buckled and fell to the floor, revealing the long crack Bekah and I had left. Although now the crack was worse and there was a large dent where Dad had hit the board.

Mom switched off the television. "Samuel," she shouted, "I'm not going to let you watch football if you're going to break things."

Dad stormed up to his room and Mom followed soon after. The rest of us sat there in shock. "Dad broke it," James said, staring at the ironing board in disbelief.

"No, we broke it," I admitted. "Dad just made it worse."

"Does Mommy know you broke it?" James asked.

"No."

"Are you going to tell her?"

"Not right now," Bekah said quickly. "They're not happy as it is. That would just make them even more mad and then they'd be mad at us."

"They'd be mad at you," Eliza corrected. "We didn't break the ironing board. You and Jessica did."

"Shut up," I hissed.

Eliza pouted and we turned our attention back to the television, which I had turned on so that we could watch the game. Just because Dad was in trouble didn't mean the rest of us should miss out. I turned it on just in time to see BYU make a touchdown. We all cheered and I went upstairs and gingerly knocked on the door.

"Who is it?" Mom's voice asked.

"Jessica."

"What do you want?"

"I just wanted to let Daddy know that BYU scored. They're ahead now."

There was silence for a moment. "Thank you, Jessica. We'll be downstairs in a moment. Would you please get out some tortilla chips for your father and the salsa?"

"Yes, Mom."

And so it was that Dad took the fall for yet another misdeed that his children were responsible for. Now, no one can say that he didn't make the problem worse. The crack Bekah and I had put into it probably could have been worked around, maybe even fixed. Nothing could take the large dent out of it though. When Mom and Dad came back downstairs, a big bowl of tortilla chips and dip bowl of salsa waiting for Dad, they were both smiling and the game ended fairly peacefully with BYU taking the victory. "Was it really worth the ironing board, sweetie?" Mom teased him as they sat talking about the game.

"Hey, you told me the other day that you wanted a new one," Dad retorted with a sheepish smile. "I was just ensuring that you got one sooner rather than later."

Mom laughed and kissed Dad's cheek. Yeah, Dad got in trouble for us, but you can't say it didn't end well for him anyway.

Fire Drill

Nothing is worse than being told on a gorgeous spring day that you can't go outside. Especially if there is no logical reason for you not to be outside enjoying the beautiful weather. Such a thing can lead to mutiny and riot. Or, as in our case, it can lead to sneaky and creative ways of escaping the house that you as a parent would not have thought of. Bekah could take anything apart, and often put it back together. And so it was that after being told we had to stay inside, despite the fact that it wasn't Sunday, Bekah learned how to pop the screen out of the boys' room window. Now the boys' room is on the upstairs level of our split level home. It had started innocently enough. We were playing one of our favorite games of make-believe, flying bed. We could go anywhere in the world we wanted to. The window was open to let the nice breeze through the house, though we had closed the door when Mom had said she wanted to take a nap. Bekah kept fiddling with the screen.

"You're going to break that," I warned.

"No I'm not, I'm just going to see if I can move it," she retorted.

I rolled my eyes and the rest of us started building with the Legos. Soon Bekah gave a little cry of triumph.

"Look, I did it!" she said.

I looked over and the window screen had been popped out. "Bekah," I hissed, trying to keep my voice down so Mom wouldn't hear me. She was taking a nap in the room next door. "You're going to get in huge trouble. Where's the screen?"

"Well, that's the only problem," she said, pointing out the window.

I stuck my head out. There on the ground was the screen, the frame slightly bent. "Great, that's really great. How do you plan on getting it back, genius?"

"I'm going to jump out the window," Bekah replied.

"What?" I gulped.

"I'm going to jump out the window."

"Can I do it too?" Eliza asked.

"No," I said just as Bekah said, "Sure."

"Are you nuts? You'll get hurt," I snapped.

"No I won't. It's not that far down. Watch." And before I could do anything to stop her, Bekah jumped out the window.

"That looks like fun," James said.

"Don't even think about it," I replied.

"But Eliza's doing it too," he pouted. I turned and sure enough, Eliza was disappearing out the window. Bekah helped her back to her feet.

"Are you two okay?" I asked.

"We're fine, it's not that far down and it doesn't hurt at all. Come on," Bekah beckoned. "If you toss Steven out, I'll catch him and then he won't get hurt."

I admit, it was very tempting. The breeze ruffled my hair and tickled my nose. It was so beautiful out and Mom hadn't given any good reason for us not to go outside. Maybe just a few minutes out wouldn't hurt. "Okay, but don't miss him. If he falls and breaks his neck

Mom will kill us." I picked Steven up. "My tun?" he asked.

"Yep, your turn."

"No way! Steven doesn't get to go before me," James said and jumped out the window. "Wee!" he cried.

"Now my tun?"

"Yes, Steven, now it's your turn." I waited until Bekah was directly below me. I leaned out of the window as far as I could without falling out, which terrified me. I knew if I fell out on top of Bekah and Steven there would be three of us hurt and I could kiss ever getting to do anything fun again goodbye. Bekah reached her arms up and could almost grab him from me. I let him drop into her arms and he giggled. They moved out of the way and I jumped down, landing easily on my feet. I stood straight up and grabbed the window screen off the ground. "You bent the frame," I told Bekah.

She waved a hand. "It'll bend back easily enough," she said. "Those things are so flimsy anyway. Not at all well-built. If I was going to do it…"

"If you were going to do it, you wouldn't bother," I interrupted. "How would you jump out of your windows?"

"Good point."

We ran around the yard for a while and played around our favorite tree. After a while I realized that if we didn't go inside soon, Mom would wake up and find that we weren't in the boys' room playing anymore. "We better go back inside."

"Yeah, I hadn't thought of how we would do that."

"Well, the door's unlocked; we could just walk back inside."

"No, that's a really bad idea. What if Mom is awake and downstairs?" Bekah asked.

"I hadn't thought of that," I admitted. "What do you think we should do?"

"Well, we jumped out. We can just climb back in," Eliza said.

"How?"

"Like this," James said. We looked over. He had climbed onto the decorative siding outside the window by stepping first onto the porch and then around the bushes onto the siding. He pulled himself onto one piece, then another before climbing back in through the open window. "See? It's easy!"

"I bet I can do that," Eliza said and started up the same way. Soon she was inside too. Then Bekah went up. Her feet slipped a few times, but after a while she was able to get inside too.

"Hand Steven to me. I think I can reach him if you lean him from the porch."

"I'll try, but I don't know that I can lean that far," I said. I picked Steven up.

"I don wanna go."

"I'm sorry, kiddo, we have to."

Steven pouted at me, but let me hold him up. I leaned as far as I could and Bekah reached. "This isn't going to work," she said. "But I could almost reach him when you tossed him down. Maybe if you stand there and toss him up…"

"Or you could see if Mom's still sleeping and I could just walk inside from the front door," I said. "I think my feet are too big to slide across the siding anyway."

"What if she's awake?"

"Just tell her you're going to check the mail and open the door and we'll sneak in."

"Okay." Bekah disappeared for a moment before coming back to the window. "She's still sleeping. Come on in."

I opened the front door and walked into the house. Carrying Steven upstairs, I didn't think about how stupid we had just been or the fact that someone could have gotten hurt if they hadn't landed right. Instead I thought about how much fun that had been and couldn't wait until we tried it again. After setting Steven down inside, I went back out long enough to grab the screen and brought it back upstairs where everyone was playing with Legos again. Bekah put the screen back in place, though there was a side that never quite bent totally back into place. "Oops," she shrugged. "I bet Mom and Dad won't even notice. Usually this window is closed anyway.

For several months we got away with jumping out of the window to sneak outside to play. Eliza and James got better and better at climbing back in and soon it would become a race between them. They would jump outside, run around the house and then climb back in. Bekah and I were their timers. Bekah had gotten good enough at removing the screen that she could pull it inside rather than just knocking it out. Steven thought it vastly unfair that we never allowed him to jump by himself. "I a big boy," he would pout.

"We just don't want you to get hurt," I would reply and kiss the top of his head. This never satisfied him, but he didn't try to do it himself. He would just pout at me as I dropped him down to Bekah.

Then one day, unbeknownst to us, the neighbor across the street happened to be looking out her window as we began another jumping escapade. Panicked, she called our house and Mom answered the phone. "Did you know your children are jumping out the window?" she asked before Mom could even finish saying hello.

Mom hadn't known, but wasn't about to admit to it. "Oh, yes, they're just practicing their fire drill," she said. "We've been talking about fire safety this month with our kids."

"I just wanted to make sure you knew. That's very dangerous; especially for the littlest one."

"Has Steven jumped out the window?" Mom asked.

"Well, no, the older ones dropped him to each other."

"Oh, good, that means they're doing what we want them to do. Sam is watching them, so we know they're alright." Dad gave Mom an odd look while she continued, "Alright, thanks for calling." Before Dad could ask what the call was about, Mom said, "Sam, go to the door and tell the kids to race to the mailbox and back."

"But they're upstairs," Dad said.

"No, apparently they're outside. But go do that now."

As we were playing, suddenly Dad showed up at the doorway. We stopped what we were doing and stared at him. "Alright, kids, go race to the mailbox and then come back to me. Who can do it the fastest?"

That got us moving and we ran to the mailbox and then back to the house. When we got inside Mom was waiting. "Well?" she asked in that tone that told us she knew something was up.

"We got bored?" James tried smiling winningly.

"What if you had gotten hurt?" Mom asked

"How did you even get outside in the first place?" Dad demanded.

Five heads looked down at the floor. "We jumped out the window," I said quietly.

Steven looked up and smiled. "It fun!"

Mom shook her head and Dad stared at us. "Fun? My children who won't climb ladders and who won't do things that are up high will jump out of windows and think it's fun?"

"We're sorry," I said.

"Just don't do it again," Mom told us. "Someone could get hurt doing that and I don't want the neighbors calling again because my children are jumping out windows."

"She saw us?"

"Yes, and you scared her half to death," Mom said.

We couldn't help but grin a little bit. "We won't do it again."

"Good. I covered for you this time, but don't expect me to do it twice. Go back upstairs and play. And Rebekah, I want you to put that screen back on the window."

"Yes, Mom," she said quietly. She knew she was in trouble when her full name was used.

I'd love to tell you that from then on we didn't jump out the window, but that would be lying. We just made sure that we waited until a time that the neighbors were away before doing it. Although, this stage of jumping out the window didn't last for very long; mostly because it became impossible for any of us to climb back using the siding. For one thing, the bushes that had been planted under the window grew to the point that we couldn't get around them to get to the siding. The second problem was we all kept growing. I had never been able to keep my balance on the skinny wood pieces because my feet were simply too big. But soon Bekah and Eliza couldn't keep their toes on the pieces either. James was the only one who it didn't seem to matter how much he grew. But as we grew too big to get back in the way we got out, the game stopped. It wasn't worth getting caught. We'd escaped trouble once because Mom believed in allowing us to learn from our own mistakes. But we all knew that if we repeated the mistake and got caught doing it, we weren't going to get away with it.

The Park of Doom

Just past our neighborhood was a park. It was a small, wooded area with a bridge perfect for playing bridge trolls, a slide, dump truck, and a merry-go-round. We didn't go to Woodlawn Park often because it tended to make Mom a little nervous. There was a bike jump course and a lot of older kids hung out there. However if it was early in the afternoon, Mom didn't mind us going too much. "But if anyone else comes, I want you to come home," she would tell us.

One day when we were over there, we decided to play on the merry-go-round. Now, you should know that I am extremely clumsy. How I escaped worse injury than I received I think is due to overly-diligent guardian angels. I owe them a huge apology for all the scrapes I got myself into. I'm sure the other angels in heaven knew exactly which ones were mine. "Oh, what'd she do today?" I can see them asking sympathetically as my poor guardian comes hobbling in bruised and beaten.

On that day my guardian angel would have replied, "Merry-go-round."

Since I was the biggest, it was almost always my job to push the merry-go-round. My siblings were very good about holding on to the poles and staying there until the merry-go-round stopped. Me? Well, there's a reason my poor angel got battered and bruised a lot. I wasn't the smartest kid around. The younger kids had decided they wanted to go play in the sand pit with the dump truck. Bekah and I were still playing on the merry-go-round.

"I bet I can walk across while this is moving," I told her as we sat on it.

"You can't walk across. You're too clumsy when it's not moving. You'll fall down," Bekah said.

"Will not."

"Will too."

"Will not."

"Prove it!"

So I started the merry-go-round and jumped on. Once I was sure I had my balance, I started walking across. I was doing pretty good until I got to the middle. Then as I took another step, I lost my footing and crashed into one of the poles, hitting my elbow.

"I told you so!" Bekah cried triumphantly. She laughed for a little while and then noticed that I was crying. "Are you okay?"

"I hit my arm really hard and it hurts," I replied.

"Well, it can't be too bad," Bekah said. "You'll probably just have another bruise to add to your collection.

"We should head home," I sniffed. "It hurts to bend it."

"That's not good," Bekah told me and hopped down from the merry-go-round.

I walked over to the sand pit where Eliza, James and Steven were still playing. "We need to go home."

"But we're still playing," James whined.

"Jessica hurt herself and we need to let Mom see it," Bekah said.

The others pouted a little, but took our hands like they were supposed to when we were out and we started the walk home. Eliza and James held onto Bekah's hands and Steven held my left hand while I kept my right arm bent the same way I had hit it. I had just learned in Young Women that if you thought something was broken, you should try not to move it. The whole walk home I knew I was in for big trouble. Mom had told me a million times not to try stunts like that. Now I was going to have a broken arm because I didn't listen to her. Tears trickled down my cheeks as we walked. Steven squeezed my hand. "I lu- oo, Je-ee-ja."

I smiled through my tears at him. "I love you too, Steven."

"Okay?" he asked.

"I'll be fine."

When we got home, Bekah announced as we walked in the door, "Jessica walked across the merry-go-round while it was moving and hurt her arm."

I scowled at her.

"Let me see," Mom said. She had me sit down at the table and started looking at my arm. "What were you doing, Jessica?" she asked.

"Walking across the merry-go-round," I said, my head hanging.

"Was that a good idea?"

"No."

"Where did you hit it?" she asked.

"Right under my elbow. It hurts a lot," I told her.

She gingerly felt around the large bruise forming on my arm and then frowned. "Samuel," she called. "I need you down here, please."

Dad knew that if Mom used his full name either he was in trouble or something was wrong. He came quickly down from their room and said, "What do you need?"

"Does she have a hot spot?" Mom asked, moving so Dad could sit down where she had been. "I can't quite tell because the whole area is warm from that bruise."

Dad gently felt around my arm. I winced as he touched the spot just under my elbow. He frowned too and I knew this was going to be bad. "We better take her to Dr. Martin. I think that is a hot spot."

"Do you want me to take her and you can watch the others? I'm sure they'll let me borrow a phone if it's anything very serious."

"Sure," Dad said.

Mom took me to the car and we drove down to the family clinic. Dr. Martin soon came and said, "So, what did you do, Jessica?"

"I fell and hit my arm on the merry-go-round pole."

"How did you do that?"

I blushed. "I was walking while it was moving."

"Hmm," he said as he started looking at my arm. "Well, I'd say you learned your lesson, right?"

I nodded.

"Well, there's definitely a hot spot there. Let's do an x-ray and we'll see what we need to do. If she broke it in the right spot, we'll be able to just set it here and get it taken care of. But, she may have broken it at the growth plate, in which case you'll have to take her to the hospital for pins and to be set."

"Pins?" I asked. That didn't sound good at all.

"Don't worry. Let's do that x-ray."

Soon Mom and I were waiting for him to come back. It seemed to be taking an awfully long time to just look at an x-ray. When Dr. Martin finally came back in he was frowning. "Jessica, I should be setting your arm right now. I just want you to know that."

"Is it broken badly?" I asked glumly.

"No, it's not broken at all! I've had every single doctor here look at this x-ray," he said, putting it up on the wall so Mom and I could see it. "Every single one because you have a hot spot and your arm should be broken. But do you see any breaks?"

"No?" I said, feeling confused. It was kind of weird looking at my bones.

"No, not even a hairline fracture," he complained. "You better thank God for your angels and send them a big thank you, young lady. Because one of them probably broke his arm keeping yours in one piece." He turned to

Mom. "Give her an ice pack to prevent swelling, but other than that she's fine."

It was a long time before any of us ventured to Woodlawn Park again. The next time anyone did, though, was the last time. Bekah had a friend over and asked Mom if we could go over to the park.

"Bekah, it rained a lot yesterday, it's probably too muddy for you to play today," Mom said.

"Please, Mom? Please? We won't get in the mud at all, I promise," Bekah said. "If there's any mud, we'll come straight home."

Mom hesitated for a moment, but with five pairs of big eyes pointed at her she finally caved in. "Alright, if you promise to stay out of the mud and come home if there is any, then you can go to the park to play. Which park are you going to?"

"Woodlawn Park," Bekah replied.

"I'd rather you went to the school playground," Mom said.

"But we haven't been to Woodlawn Park in forever," Bekah argued.

"Alright, that's fine. Jessica, will you go with them?"

"I don't want to go to the park today. I've got homework," I replied. Actually, my not wanting to go had nothing to do with homework. The last time I had gone to Woodlawn Park I had nearly broken my arm and I had no intention of going back.

"Well then the rest of you can go. Steven, James and Eliza, you hold their hands and do what they tell you to. And remember, if there is any mud you come straight home," Mom said.

"Okay, Mom," they said and out they went. Bekah told me later what had happened when they got there. Our favorite place to play at the park was near the bridge, but with all the rain Bekah was sure that it would be too muddy to play over there. But to her surprise, when they got there it looked completely dry. "Hey, let's play bridge trolls," Bekah said.

"That'll be fun," Eliza said. "Can I be the first troll?"

"Sure," Bekah replied.

Eliza stepped out and yelped as she sank waist-high in mud. "Help!" she cried.

James and Steven both started trying to grab her arms and they were soon just as deep in the muck.

"Mom's going to kill us," Bekah moaned as she and her friend started trying desperately to pull the three younger kids out of the mud. It was quite some time before the five of them were all out of the mud and standing far from the mud pit. "It's just not fair," Bekah said as they stared at what had looked dry and was now oozing and wet. "It looked completely dry."

"What should we do?" her friend asked.

"There's only one thing we can do," Bekah said, squaring her shoulders and ready for the trouble that was about to ensue. "We go home. We promised that if there was any mud we'd go straight home."

"But we also promised to stay out of the mud," Eliza pointed out.

"Yeah, I know," Bekah said. "All we can do is tell Mom the truth and hope she believes us." She then took hold of Steven's hand and he took Eliza's. James took Bekah's other hand and the five of them began their death march towards the house. Several people who knew us saw them on the way.

"Why don't you stop at my house and I'll hose you down?" one person offered. "You might dry off some before you get home."

"No, we'll just tell Mom the truth," Bekah replied gloomily.

Several others offered to hose them down or just to bring out washcloths for their faces and hands. Each time Bekah told them no. She always was the most honest of all of us. When they got to the house, I was outside because Mom had asked me to check the mail. I burst out laughing. "You are so going to die!" I laughed.

"Thanks a lot, jerk," Bekah retorted. "Would you please get Mom?"

There was no need to. Mom had been getting ready to leave for a bit anyway. When she came outside, the five muddy children were standing in a row looking so forlorn and dejected that a hint of a smile played on Mom's face. "Rebekah, what happened?" she asked, keeping her voice stern.

Bekah looked at the ground. "The ground looked dry under the bridge, so we went to play there. I guess it wasn't dry all the way." She looked up at Mom pleadingly. "It really was an accident. We didn't mean to break our promise."

At last, Mom couldn't contain herself anymore. She laughed, "Well, have Jessica hose you guys off and bring towels to you before you come inside. Then get into fresh clothes and we'll see about your friend staying the night."

"Really?" Bekah asked.

"Really. Next time I say it's too muddy, how about we stay at home, okay?" Mom said with a smile.

"Okay."

And that was the last time we went to Woodlawn Park. Part of this was due to Mom forbidding it when there started to be rumors about what some of the teenagers were doing there. But we didn't ask to go back either. With having two horrible experiences there close together we had decided that the park was cursed. From that point on if we wanted to play at a park, we went to the school playground where Mom knew we would be safe and where we had never had any accidents.

Surprises

I'd love to tell you that as the oldest in my family I was the leader, but that would be false. Bekah was the true leader in our group. I was always her second in command and sometimes she was generous enough to allow me to think that I was the leader for the day. But the truth of the matter is that Bekah is a natural leader and can get people to follow her. I'm just oldest-child-bossy. You know the type if you have older siblings. It's that attitude of "I'm bigger than you and older than you, so you're going to do what I say because I said so." My siblings didn't fall for it often, not that it stopped me from trying. But Bekah had a way of saying exactly the same thing I did, sometimes in the exact same way, and the rest of my siblings would follow her. At first this caused a lot of contention between us because, well, I'm the oldest. I should be in charge and they should listen to me. Then I saw the advantages of her talent. If Bekah and

I joined forces, we could get our siblings to do just about anything.

Sometimes when Mom and Dad were gone we actually wanted to do things that would surprise them in a good way. Usually it was something for an anniversary or just because. One year their anniversary fell on a Sunday and we decided that since they couldn't go out on a date we would bring the date to them. Bekah and I planned how we were going to do it. Mom and Dad for some reason were going to be having an extra meeting that Sunday, so that would give us time to set things up. We made up assignments: Eliza was to clear the table off and set out the dishes just for Mom and Dad. James was in charge of making Mom's candlesticks look extra shiny (sorry, Mom, I think he may have spit on them) and help get the silverware set out. Steven was to put the candles on the candlesticks. Bekah and I were the chefs. Bekah made the salad and the Kool-Aid and I made the grilled cheese sandwiches. I was also in charge of slicing the apples since the others weren't quite big enough to use the knives yet. I made our dinner first so that Mom wouldn't have to make anything for us and we would already be fed so they could eat by themselves. Then we waited for Mom and Dad to get home and the younger three decorated menus for Mom and Dad. While we were waiting, we cleaned the kitchen, the dining room and the living room. Steven was the look-out, watching at the window for Mom and Dad to get home.

"Dey hee," he cried.

"Quick, everyone but Bekah needs to go upstairs!" I said.

The three youngest scrambled up the stairs. Bekah was going to be our waitress so she stood by the door waiting for them to come inside. I grabbed a box of matches from the top of the cupboard and lit the candles just before Bekah welcomed them in. "Welcome Madam and Sir to our restaurant."

"What's going on?" Dad asked.

"We heard that you have a special occasion today and have prepared a special meal for you," Bekah continued. "Will you follow me to your seats please?" Mom and Dad followed her and sat down at the table.

She handed them their menus. "What can I get for you to drink?"

"It looks like we only have one option," Dad said.

"Would you like Kool-aid?" Bekah asked.

Mom nodded and gave Dad a look. "Sure," he said.

She left them and got the glasses from me and put a few ice cubes in each one. Then she returned. "And what would you like for your meal today?"

"We'll both have grilled cheese sandwiches and a salad please," Mom smiled.

Bekah wrote it down on a post-it note. "I'll be right back with those." She came into the kitchen and I handed her the plates. She took them back and said, "Enjoy your meal. If you need anything just yell. We'll be in the office."

"The office?" Dad asked.

"That's the boys' room, Dad," I explained quietly. Then Bekah and I turned around and went upstairs, leaving them to a probably very unromantic anniversary dinner. But at our age that was the best we could do.

For their fifteenth anniversary, we decided we wanted to do something fun. After all, fifteen years is an awfully long time when you're young. I had saved some of my babysitting money and bought a couple of plain white tee-shirts. Using my very best hand writing, I wrote on the front "Happy 15th Anniversary!" with fabric puff paint. I drew little stick people underneath to represent Mom and Dad. Then I had each of my siblings come into the room I was working in. I squeezed some fabric paint into their hands, told them to rub it all over the front and then had them place their handprints on the shirts in the shape of a heart. I labeled each handprint heart with the proper name. Then we set them in the downstairs bathroom to dry. Mom and Dad never used that bathroom, so we knew they'd be safe there at least long enough for the paint to dry.

We had been watching a movie about time capsules and I looked at Bekah, "Hey, wouldn't it be cool if we put Mom and Dad's shirts into a time capsule and buried it in the backyard?"

"Yeah, but what if they find it too soon?"

"How often have you seen Mom and Dad digging in the backyard?" I asked. "Really? It would be fine. Besides, we've got tons of plastic bins that we don't use anymore. We'll just put the shirts and some things to help them remember all the things we've done together. It would be so cool. And we could make it like a treasure hunt by giving them different clues on how to find it."

"Or we could draw a map!" Bekah exclaimed.

"What are you girls up to in there?" Mom asked from the kitchen.

"Nothing!" we said at once.

The next time Mom and Dad were gone, we put together the box of memories and tee-shirts. Then we went outside to the backyard and started digging a hole to put it in. After what seemed forever, the hole was finally deep enough to put the box into. We set it down and started covering it up again with dirt. Satisfied that our time capsule was well-hidden, we went back inside. We weren't in for very long before Bekah said, "Jessica, what if someone steals our time capsule?"

"Why would anyone want to steal our time capsule?" I asked her.

"Well, those neighbors over there are kind of mean. They may have watched us put it in and decided to steal it just to be mean."

I rolled my eyes. "I'm sure it'll be fine."

"Well, what if it rains and water gets into the lid?" Bekah argued. "We didn't put anything around that lid to seal it up."

"I guess that's a good point. Maybe we should dig it up."

"We could hide it in the linen closet behind all the old sheets. None of us ever get stuff from down there. And we could still make clues or a map that Mom and Dad have to follow in order to get it."

"Good idea." So Bekah and I went back outside while the others continued to watch the movie inside. We dug up the time capsule, breaking the lid with the shovel as we did. At first we panicked thinking that someone else had tried to dig up our box, but the panic didn't last long.

"I bet we did that while digging it up," Bekah admitted sheepishly.

"Well, let's wash the dirt off of this and stick it in the closet."

"Right."

The weeks that followed seemed to drag on and on until Mom and Dad's anniversary. Bekah and I decided that the next time we decided to plan something fun, we should do it only a few days before their anniversary rather than a couple months. Mom and Dad had no idea that there was a box of memories and gifts waiting in the closet. But we were going insane waiting for them to be able to go through the series of clues we'd made for them.

Finally their anniversary arrived. Dad had the day off and for the morning we played games and spent time together as a family. During one of the last games, while I put up the clues for Mom and Dad's treasure hunt, Bekah couldn't stand the suspense anymore. "We have a present for you," she announced.

"Really? Where is it?" Mom asked.

"You have to find it," I replied. "We've made up a bunch of clues and this is the first one." I handed her a piece of paper.

Now, I have to give my parents a huge wave of credit right now. Every time we came up with some scheme to surprise them, they always played along. Even though our surprise dinners were never fancy or truly special, they played along. When we made up games, they played along. And this was no different; they went through various rooms of the house looking for the clues until they finally arrived at the linen closet and pulled out all of the old sheets. Dad pulled out the plastic box with its cracked and dented lid. Then we all went downstairs so that we could watch Mom and Dad open it. As they did, we watched with excitement. They pulled out the little memories we had written down, Mom reading them. Then they pulled out their matching tee-shirts.

"Do you like them?" I asked nervously.

Dad pulled his shirt over the one he was already wearing. "They're great, kids. Thank you."

"Happy anniversary!" we all called.

Mom and Dad smiled. "Thanks, kids. This was the best anniversary present ever."

Stuck in a Tree

Most of our favorite games were played outside. Our yard wasn't huge, but it was big enough for all sorts of adventures. We could hide behind the bushes in the backyard for hide-and-seek or we liked to play in the shadows of our garage on the driveway. We played a dinosaur game where the cars driving past were dinosaurs and if you were still out in the sunshine when they drove past, you got eaten. It was a fun game and was played often on spring and summer days. We also enjoyed playing football and tag since there was plenty of room to run around in. And if you hadn't already figured it out, we're a pretty physical bunch.

If we were bored with our yard, we would ask Mom if we could walk to the school playground. The school playground, as it was when I was in school, had multiple places where games of make-believe were easy to play. There was a large play area that had two slides, a ship's wheel, and a climbing area built of tires. It was also attached to monkey bars and rings which made it perfect for turning into a really interesting pirate ship. If we had recently watched *Shipwrecked!*, we found ourselves battling against pirates and racing them to the buried treasure. On the other hand, if *Treasure Island* had been the most recent pirate movie, we were the pirates trying to outwit everyone else. Bekah was our captain and I her willing first mate.

"Weigh anchor!" she would yell as we played.

"Aye, aye, captain," I would salute. "You heard the captain. Weigh anchor!"

The game would continue often long after we were supposed to head home. There were only a few times that Mom got worried and came driving over in the van to pick us up. Otherwise she would just wait patiently at home for us to arrive. "Do you know how long you were gone?" she'd ask as we come in.

"An hour?" I'd reply hopefully.

She'd shake her head.

"Two hours?"

"You need to take some kind of watch with you to keep track of the time. I was starting to get worried," Mom would say. "You've been gone for a long time."

In another section of the playground was an area of equipment with a spider web of ropes and a large area enclosed by uneven, raised logs. That was our favorite place to play lava monster. If you have never played that before, your childhood has been seriously lacking! One of us would be the monster and the others would try to get around the logs without falling onto the sand. If you fell in, you became the new lava monster. Occasionally the lava monster would be generous enough to give you ten seconds to find a new spot before trying to pull you down. The spider web was a good place to play just about anything. After I read *The Lord of the Rings*, it quickly became Shelob's lair and we often reenacted our favorite scenes from the epic tale. The tallest slide became Lothlorien and other parts of the playground received whatever location was most fitting.

But our favorite playground equipment was a small wooden set. It also had a ship's wheel in the front part and then to make it even better had a sail-shaped wooden part that you could sit in. That part was often used by children during cold recesses as shelter against Kansas winter winds. I remember several recesses spent huddled with five to six other children in that wooden sail. But when I was there with my siblings, that piece of equipment was either a small pirate ship or, even more fun, a time machine. We used the wheel to spin ourselves through time back to the age of dinosaurs, to ancient Egypt, to the Renaissance, to Neil Armstrong's famous moonwalk; whatever period in history most interested us that day. We battled knights, ran from velociraptors, and sailed down the Nile all from that toy.

Often though, we stayed at home and got into mischief in our own yard. The cottonwood in our front yard was perfect for climbing into. It was right next to the fence to the backyard which gave us the start we needed to get to the lowest branches. At first, Bekah and I were the only ones who could get up there, but soon Eliza, James and Steven had grown enough that they could climb into the tree too. It's a little disappointing that the tree died and was cut down before John was ever able to climb up into it. But the rest of us did this quite often; despite Mom telling us several times that she didn't want us climbing it. How could we resist? The fence made the perfect step-ladder into the lowest branches and then it was just a matter of going as high as you were comfortable going. Bekah and I tended to stay on the lowest branches, suffering a little from fear of heights. We would bring out our favorite books and climb into the tree with them to read. Many balmy afternoons were spent in those branches, the adventure of some new story taking us to far-away places. Eliza would usually just climb up and act as our lookout. She wasn't interested in taking her books into the tree like Bekah and I did, though occasionally she would. James and Steven, however, were the monkeys. They would climb higher and higher until they got as high as they could go before shouting down to Bekah and I, "Look at me!"

"Come back down here," I would tell them. "You're too high up. You could fall and get hurt."

Usually they were quick to scurry back down the tree. But there was one afternoon that they were climbing and I realized that it was time for us to go inside. "Alright, everyone climb back down," I said. "We need to go back inside."

Bekah and I hopped down from the limbs we'd been sitting on with the books we were reading. Eliza clambered out of the tree and down the fence to the ground. James was also quick about coming out of the tree. I realized that the only one left up in the tree was Steven. "Steven, come on, we need to go inside," I said looking back up.

I was answered with a scared whimper. Steven was clutching a limb at least twenty-five feet up in the air. "I can't," he cried. "I'm scared."

Steven had never gotten scared climbing into the tree before. I don't know if he'd never looked down before or if he'd just gone up higher than he ever had before. But I knew that he was going to need help. I gulped. "Alright, kiddo, give me a second. I'm going to climb up to you and help you come down."

"Okay. Hurry!"

I climbed back up the fence and into the tree. I took a deep breath as I went up higher and higher. I was probably about fifteen feet up when the next branch I stepped onto began to creak under my weight. I knew that it would be dangerous for me to go any higher. "Steven, I can't get any closer to you. I need you to come down to me."

"I'm too scared, Jessica. Can't you come and get me?"

I sighed. "Steven, I'm too big to get where you are. I won't let you fall, come down to me."

"I can't."

James shouted up, "I'll help you, Steven."

Before I could argue with him, James was scurrying up the tree to Steven's position. I climbed back down and stood just under where the boys were in case one of them fell. "Don't worry, Steven, I won't let you get hurt," I called. "Just keep coming down with James."

"Okay." Together, they were coming one branch at a time. Every now and again they would stop as Steven would panic at how high up he was.

"It's okay," James would say to him. "I'm right here and I won't let you fall. I promise. Just come one more branch. Do it like me."

Soon they were both down on the ground and Steven wrapped himself around me. I ruffled his hair. "It's alright, kiddo. I don't like being that high up either."

"Do I have to climb the tree again?" he asked.

"No, Steven. You don't have to go into the tree again if you don't want to," I promised him.

It was a long time before Steven ventured to the tree again and when he did, he stayed on the lower branches with Bekah and I. Even James never went quite as high up again. I think we all realized that we had been a little foolish. Alright, maybe a lot foolish. Okay, so it was a really horribly bad idea. But in any case, we stayed together on the lower branches, sometimes with me reading stories aloud and sometimes just enjoying the nice weather.

Suddenly Mommy

The hardest part of being the oldest is having to fill in for a parent when they are not available to take care of things themselves. My youngest brother, John, was born on a Saturday via an emergency c-section and there were complications on top of that. That meant that while Mom was in the hospital, I was Mommy. On the Sunday after he was born, I helped get everyone dressed and ready for church. Dad had gone to the hospital early in the morning to be with Mom and John. The five of us children walked to the church building. It was only a couple of blocks away and we had walked there before on nice days. This time wasn't as pleasant since it was hot out and we were all worried about Mom and John. Even though Dad had assured us that they would be fine, the fact that we hadn't been able to see them for ourselves made us worry. Five silent Schofields walked into the building and started to go to the chapel. One of the sisters in the ward saw us and said, "Jessica, where are your parents? Did your mom have her baby?"

"Yeah, she did," I said quietly. "Bekah, can you take them to sit down?"

Bekah nodded and took the others into the chapel to our usual pew.

"Is everything okay?" the sister asked.

I shook my head and started crying as I tried to explain what Dad had told me. She hugged me and then steered me to the bishop who asked the same questions and got the same blubbering response. I think God blesses bishops, and really any church leaders, to be able to understand sobbing women. I don't think there's any other way our poor bishop could have made heads or tails of what I was saying. He asked if we needed anything and I sniffed. "I don't think so. We're just really worried, that's all."

"I understand," he said gently.

That Sunday was one of the longest we'd ever experienced. It was probably one of the Sundays that we were the best behaved too, simply because we were too preoccupied to bother misbehaving. And I think we were trying to be our best so that Mom could be proud of us when she was able to come home. When church was finally over, the same sister who had watched us walk in drove us home. She made her kids wait at the church building so that she could take us home first. "If you kids need anything at all, you call me, okay?" she said.

"Thank you, we'll do that," I told her. I then followed my brothers and sisters into the house and changed clothes before starting to make dinner. It wasn't long before there was a knock at the door and someone from church arrived carrying a covered, foil casserole dish.

"I figured you kids would be hungry and I'm sure your dad hasn't gotten anything set up for your dinner," she said as she handed it to me.

"Oh, thanks," I said. I didn't have the heart to tell her that it didn't matter that Dad hadn't planned dinner. I knew how to cook and had already started something. Instead I smiled and accepted the meal.

"Is there anything else you need right now?"

"No, I don't think so. I think we've got everything set that we need," I said.

"Well, you call if you think of anything. Have your dad call too if he thinks of something."

"I'll do that, thank you."

After I had closed the door behind her, I looked at what was in the casserole dish. It was going to be better than what I was making anyway, so I turned off the water I had started and set the dish on the stove.

It was ten days before Mom and John were allowed to come home. I suddenly went from being just a normal teenager like any other to a full-time mommy. Every morning after seminary, I would come home, wake the others and get them ready for school. I packed lunches and checked homework assignments before then double checking that I had the things that I needed as well. After school, I would walk to the elementary school to pick up James and Steven before going home. Sometimes we beat Eliza and Bekah, who were being picked up by a family friend who took over Mom's carpool for her, and sometimes we didn't. That friend would come in and stay for an hour, making sure that the others were taken care of so that I could do my homework. I will bless her name forever because if it weren't for her, I don't think I would have bothered with my own schoolwork at all. She would help me get through my math and then keep the others occupied while I did any other assignments I might have. Then when the hour was up, she'd check if we needed anything else and then head home to her own family.

During those ten days we had at least fifteen meals brought to us, many in the same day and often after I had already started making something for dinner. A couple of families called ahead to see what we needed and they ended up bringing us a family home evening lesson and game for Monday and then a game night and movie for Friday, since I told them we had far more meals than we could possibly eat on our own.

But the one night I hadn't started anything (because I knew that at some point someone would show up with one and we couldn't eat four meals in one sitting), a family showed up carrying the most awkward, disgusting meal I had ever seen in my life. Even as I opened the door and the smell of the casserole wafted in, I was pasting the smile on my face to gratefully accept it. "Let me know if you need anything," she said cheerfully as she left.

"Will do," I replied. I carried the casserole dish to the table which was already set and ready for dinner.

Steven, who has always been the pickiest eater in our family, wrinkled his nose. "I am not eating that."

"Me neither," James said.

Bekah and Eliza started nodding in agreement.

"Now, we should be very thankful that someone was being kind enough to bring us a meal. They didn't have to do it," I said, trying to channel my best Mommy voice.

"I can't even tell what that is," Bekah said. "I'm not going to eat it if I don't know what it is."

"Bekah, you're not helping," I muttered.

"Look at it!"

"I know!" I exclaimed, feeling exasperated. Dad had given me forty dollars on Monday, telling me that it was only for groceries and necessities. Since we hadn't needed anything and I figured that he would do the same thing in my shoes, I said, "Alright, here's what we're going to do. I have the money that we can order a pizza, but," I added as four pairs of hungry and excited eyes turned towards me, "everyone has to take one bite of the casserole that we were brought. She worked very hard to bring us a meal so that we wouldn't have to worry about cooking and we're going to each take a bite so that we can show we're grateful for it."

"But I'm not grateful for it," Steven argued.

"Steven, one bite won't kill you," I said sternly. "We're going to each have one bite or there won't be any pizza."

Five forks went into the casserole dish and then into mouths. Steven took as teeny-tiny a portion as he possibly could. Even Eliza, who is the best eater, only took about half a forkful. Then we were all chewing and forcing ourselves to swallow. I'm not sure what the casserole was supposed to be, but it was really bad. As soon as everyone had swallowed their one bite, I recovered the casserole dish, set it on the stove and called Pizza Hut to order a large pizza and breadsticks.

Dad got home late that night. I was still awake, finishing up an assignment that I hadn't quite been able to get done while Sheila was over. The empty breadstick box was out on the stove as Dad came over to the kitchen table to check on me. "Jessica, did someone bring over pizza?"

"Not exactly," I said, looking up from my homework. "I ordered pizza for us tonight."

"Jessica," Dad said, his voice tired and irritated, "I told you the money I left was only for groceries and necessities. Pizza is not a necessity."

"I know that, Dad, but one of the sisters brought us some sort of awkward casserole and I have no idea what it's supposed to be. I saved it in the fridge if you want to eat it, but I can guarantee you the rest of us won't. I'm so proud of Steven for taking a micro-nibble of it. I think he only did that though because I promised pizza if he did."

"You could have made something different, Jessica."

"I know, but I kind of panicked when everyone at the table started refusing to eat. Besides, we saved you some and it's your favorite," I added with a winning smile.

Dad rubbed his eyes and chuckled a little. "Oh, alright, but next time just make something up or eat what you've been brought." He opened the fridge to pull out the pizza box. He uncovered one corner of the casserole dish and his nose wrinkled a little. "This is what you were brought?"

"Yeah, pretty awful looking isn't it?" I said. "It smells better now that it's cold. When it was hot it smelled terrible."

He gave me a stern look, though there was an amused twinkle in his eye. "Be nice."

"I was," I retorted. I stretched my arms over my head and looked once more at the paper I'd been working on. "I'll finish this before seminary. I can't think anymore." I walked over to Dad and gave him a hug. "Love you, Daddy."

"Love you too, kiddo. Get some sleep."

Toilet Trouble

I've discovered that kids either fear the toilet because of the weird gurgling sound when it flushes or they think it's the greatest toy ever invented. I'm sure by now you can guess which group my family fell into. The toilet was never something scary and our toilet saw some weird stuff. All toilets that are used by a family will probably see washcloths, rubber duckies, tub toys and other normal bathroom paraphernalia. But our toilet was exposed to more than just the normal. For example, we discovered that if you took a marker apart and stuck the ink pad inside the toilet, the water would suck the ink out and the pad would puff up to double or triple its size. It would also give a tie-dyed look to the ink pad. The more pads you stuck in the water, the more interesting the color the toilet water would become. It left unusual color rings around the inside of the toilet and we had to make sure that we always cleaned it before Mom got home to see what we'd done.

The Christmas after I turned twelve, my grandmother sent me two frocked ponies. She knew I loved horses and thought they would be the perfect gift for me. And they were. I loved brushing their manes and tails and rubbing the soft fur on their sides. I gave them a special place in my bedroom and forbade my siblings from ever touching them. And that was my first mistake. My second mistake was playing more with my new ponies than I did with my brothers and sisters.

Bekah came down one afternoon and asked, "Jessica, do you want to come play flying bed with us?"

"No, I'm teaching my horses dressage."

Rolling her eyes, she said, "You can bring them with you."

"No."

"Well, can I play with you? There are two horses and only one of you."

"No."

"I'll be extra careful."

"No, I don't want you touching them. As soon as I let you touch them then everyone else will find out and they'll want to touch them and they'll get messed up."

"I won't tell anyone."

"No."

"Please?"

"NO!"

As I turned back to my horses, Bekah glared at my back and went upstairs. Instead of playing a game like they had planned, they plotted how they were going to end my fascination with the frocked ponies.

The next day I had a Young Women activity. So while I was gone, Bekah, James and Eliza took my beloved frocked ponies upstairs. Steven was in the bath at the time and Bekah offered to help him so that Mom could do some work in the study downstairs. While he was playing in the tub water, the others began bathing my horses in the toilet. First only a small section of the furry skin began to peel away, but when this was discovered, they were soon pulling long chunks of fur off. They were fascinated.

When I got home, the younger two were sitting on the couch pulling the last pieces off the creamy white plastic bodies. As I saw what they had done a fight of enormous proportions broke out. I was screaming and crying and chasing them up the stairs vowing to pull their hair out like they'd done to my horses. Luckily for them, Mom is faster than I am.

"What on earth is going on?"

"Look what they did!" I sobbed. "They ruined them!"

Mom looked at the skinned horses in James and Eliza's hands. Bits of fur clung to the plastic bodies near the face. The manes had been pulled out and so the long crack in the plastic where they had been showed. "Do you want to tell me why you did that?"

"Bekah said we were going to give the horses baths to be nice," Eliza lied.

"Rebekah," Mom said warningly as Bekah stepped out of the bathroom with Steven wrapped in a towel. "What were you doing?"

"She always played with those stupid, boring horses and she didn't ever do things with us anymore. I meant for them just to get wet. I didn't know the fur would come off."

"Did you stop when you saw it coming off?"

Bekah hung her head. "No."

"We pulled more of it off," James admitted.

"Where is the fur?"

"Flushed down the toilet," James said.

"Where?!"

"Some of it had already fallen inside the toilet, so we just flushed it down," Eliza said.

I started to puff up again and Mom said quickly, "You owe your sister an apology. Those were hers and they were expensive. You had no right to do that."

The three of them apologized and I looked at the remains of my horses. "Can we fix them?"

"No," Mom said. "You need to throw them away."

"Can't we try?"

"There's nothing I can do, Jessica. Throw them away."

I glared at my siblings through tears and took them downstairs to the trashcan. I didn't speak to any of them for the rest of the night. But I did learn my lesson. As I began collecting plastic figurines I made sure to sometimes let my siblings play with them too. And if they wanted me to go play with them, I went without argument. Never again did I get the frocked ponies, just in case.

The Nose Knows

Some children have an uncanny way of finding exactly what they aren't supposed to have. Steven had that gift for cookies. It was one of the few words that he never had any trouble pronouncing. When Mom would get special treats for the family or for Dad she would hide them in one of the cabinets in the kitchen. Even if we found the box, we knew we were to wait until later. Of course, sometimes we still snuck one or two cookies if the package had already been opened.

Mom didn't buy cookies from the store often. Usually if we wanted cookies she would bake up enough to fill our large, clear cookie jar plus some extras that would just have to be eaten right away. After all, no one wants those cookies to get lonely. But if someone had been extra good, she was in the mood or Dad was having a rough week at work Mom would buy our favorite sandwich cookies and put them in the cabinet.

Steven, like the rest of us, knew exactly where Mom hid the cookies. And somehow he always knew when she had bought cookies, even if he hadn't gone with her to the store. He would come and tug on her jeans and point up to the cupboard. "Cookie?" he would ask, using his biggest puppy eyes and most dimpled smile. She would give in almost every time and sneak out a cookie for him. "Just one," she would say. Of course, it never took long for the rest of us to see his chocolate-smeared face and want to have "just one" too.

Soon if Mom wanted the cookies to really be a surprise, she had to change her hiding spot. One afternoon while the boys were playing upstairs, Mom got home with the groceries and asked me to put them away. When I saw the cookie package (our favorite: mint), she said, "Dad's had a really awful week. Please put those in a different hiding spot than normal so that Steven doesn't find them."

"Can we have them when Daddy gets home?" I asked.

"Only when Dad gets home," she said, the warning clear in her voice. If I snuck one early, I was going to be in huge trouble.

"Aye, aye." I saluted and then put the cookies into the opposite cabinet than we usually put them in. *Steven won't find them there!* I thought.

I finished putting the rest of the groceries away as Mom came back down to start dinner. Steven came toddling after her and pointed up at the cabinet I had just put the cookies in. "Cookie peas?" he asked.

"No, sweetie, we don't have any cookies up there." Mom replied.

"Uh-huh. Cookie," he insisted.

"Steven, you know that's not where cookies go. There aren't any cookies in there for you."

His eyebrows furrowed and he started to frown. More emphatically he said, "Uh-huh. Cookie!"

Exasperated, Mom opened the cabinet. "See, Steven? There are no cookies there."

His smile returned and he pointed at the now revealed package. "Cookie! Cookie peas."

Mom looked where he was pointing and sighed. "No, Steven. Not until Daddy gets home. Those are Daddy's cookies."

"Peas?"

"Not right now."

He sniffled and bowed his head. Dad got home not long after and Steven grabbed his pantleg and started pulling him toward the cabinet. "Cookie, Da? Peas cookie?"

"Steven, we don't put cookies in that cabinet," Dad replied, a tired strain in his voice.

"Uh-huh, Da. Cookie!"

"There are cookies up there, Sam," Mom said before Dad could get into the same argument she'd had earlier. "I thought you might like a sweet treat after all the work you've been doing. Jessica tried to hide them somewhere different so Steven wouldn't find them."

Dad opened the cabinet and pulled out the cookies. "I guess the Nose knows!" he laughed. He opened the package, got out a couple of mugs and poured milk in each one. Setting a stack of cookies on the table and scooping Steven into his lap, they enjoyed some cookies together. It wasn't long before the rest of us realized there were cookies available and within minutes the package was empty.

There were many other times we tried to hide the cookies from Steven. We tried every single cabinet in the kitchen, even hiding them in the dining room hutch. Each time Steven would beeline for the hidden package and point, without opening the cabinet door, and say, "Cookie?" No matter how we tried to argue that cooies didn't belong there, or that there weren't any cookies, he never believed us.

Soon, if Mom had a treat she wanted to hide she started putting them in her underwear drawer because that was the only place none of her children would get into. I'm almost positive that Steven still knew where they were, but Mom's room was off-limits for our play and he never went to find them in there.

King of the Castle

If you're an oldest child thinking that as soon as you're an adult the blame will shift, think again. I didn't realize that the whole being a good example thing would last into college too. One weekend when I came to visit, Mom and Dad went out on a double date with our bishop and his wife. I was left in charge and soon it was just like old times. James had brought down some blankets because it was cold. As we sat watching whichever movie was John's favorite at the time, Bekah and I started talking. "You remember when we were little and we used to play pretty princesses?" she asked.

"Yeah, those were fun days. We'd get into our froofy slips…"

'You had froofy slips?" James asked, his nose wrinkled.

"Well, yeah, all slips were froofy then. So we could be princesses anytime we wanted," I said.

"And build couch castles," Bekah added

"What's a couch castle?" John asked.

"When we were little, Bekah and I used to build castles out of the couch cushions," I replied.

"Just when we were little?" she questioned with a sly grin.

"Well, when we were a bit bigger too," I admitted.

"Can I build a castle?" John asked.

"Sure, why not?" I said. In no time at all we had taken the couch apart and the cushions were precariously balanced into a castle. "Hmmm, this was a lot bigger when we were small," I told Bekah.

"Well, what if we used the landing to build a castle?" James asked.

"How?"

"It would be easy," Steven said. "All we'd have to do is use the blankets over the railings. If we used some of your hair ties and some of Dad's rope we could build an awesome castle."

Bekah and I looked at each other. "Just like old times again," she grinned.

"Yep." I smiled. "Let's get to work!"

It was probably the most impressive castle we'd ever built. It went from the upstairs landing down to the girls' landing. We attached the blankets and sheets from multiple beds together using hair ties and little pieces of rope. They were then stuck to walls and the wooden part of our couch using sewing pins and thumb tacks. The couch cushions remained a vital part of the castle, providing King John with his bedchamber. As we built and played all of us forgot about the fact that eventually Mom and Dad would come home. We also forgot that the bishop and his wife had left their car out front and then carpooled with our parents to go out.

Have you ever wished that like Mary Poppins you could snap your fingers and the mess would clean itself? Six children wished for this gift as we heard the doorknob twist. As it was, there was no way to hide the evidence of our mess as four adults walked inside.

"Look, Mommy, we built a castle!" John proclaimed proudly.

Mom's eyes flashed as she looked at me. "Jessica Lyn…"

"This is ingenious!" Bishop interrupted her. "I would never have thought to use hair ties to tie the blanket to the railing. What else did you kids do?"

Having a bishop who hasn't totally grown up yet can help keep you out of trouble…at least for a little while.

The boys excitedly explained our building process while my mother looked daggers at me. I knew we weren't getting out of it that easily. Now Mom really isn't a party-pooper. I don't think she would have cared so much if she hadn't had company with her. But she does expect us to clean up our messes before she comes home, particularly when there are guests coming as well. But in our defense, we really didn't expect the bishop and his wife to be coming inside.

"You should be engineers," Bishop told the boys, ruffling John's hair before turning back to my parents. "You've got really creative kids. We'll see you on Sunday." Then he and his wife left.

"Jessica…"

"It wasn't my idea."

"But you obviously helped," Mom said. "You're eighteen years old. You should know better by now."

"Oh, Amy, you've got to admit they were pretty creative here."

"Do not encourage them, Sam. That was embarrassing."

"Bishop didn't mind," Bekah argued. "He said we were ingenious."

Mom shook her head in defeat. "What are the rules?" she asked, looking at each of us.

"Clean the mess before you get home," we recited.

"I'm sorry, Mom," I said.

"We were going to have it cleaned up before you got home," Eliza added.

"We just lost track of time," James said.

"Get this cleaned up and everything put away and then it's bedtime."

"Do we have to go to bed?" Steven asked.

"Yes." Mom and Dad said together.

We all knew it wasn't worth the argument. So we cleaned up and Dad helped us fold up the extra blankets we'd gotten out. Then after family prayer we all said goodnight and went to our rooms for the night.

The Lip-Synching, Balancing Schofields

Our whole family loves Journey. And when I say love, I mean LOVE! Even my Dad will crank up the volume when "Don't Stop Believin'" begins. And really, we like most classic rock. One day my parents were gone all day for a temple trip. We must have listened to our Journey album ten times and each time the volume got louder and the singing along got more creative. At first we were listening and singing as we cleaned the main level of the house. Then with that done we were standing on the coffee table singing at the top of our lungs. And then Bekah had an idea. "What if we made this more challenging?"

"What do you mean?"

"Well, when the song plays, someone has to stand on top of all the couch cushions and try to sing and dance without losing their balance."

"That would be awesome!" James exclaimed.

"Well we all know I'll lose," I said. "But sure, couch cushions are soft so we probably wouldn't get hurt." Never mind the fact that there are solid wood tables, glass and crystal vases, and our large television in the living room that could have easily been hit when we fell. I think once again my overly-diligent guardian angels saved us from getting into more trouble than we could have.

And so it happened that we started piling the couch cushions in a precarious pile on the floor. The coffee table was pushed over towards the window and we put on the song. I'm not sure why it was that "Any Way You Want It" was always the song of choice. I suppose it's mostly because you can't help but groove with it. I mean really, can *you* sit still while listening to Journey? I didn't think so.

As often happened we went in age order. John, being the smallest, was allowed to use only the smallest cushions and placed as low to the ground as possible so he wouldn't fall and get hurt. The rest of us had to use all of the cushions. During one of Bekah's turns we heard over the blaring music, the sound of the door opening. One of Mom's friends walked in. She was an old family friend and had been coming in and out for so long that she never bothered knocking anymore. And she'd been asked to come check on us. As Bekah toppled to the ground and Eliza rushed to turn the music down six pairs of eyes turned towards Sally.

"Your mother asked me to check in on you," she said in a dangerously calm tone. "I will not inform her of this lunacy if, and only if, you get the couches put to right in the next thirty seconds and promise me that you will not do it again."

The couches were speedily put back together and we said together, "Sorry."

"Are you going to do it again?"

We all shook our heads.

"Do you need anything right now?"

"No."

"Jessica, have you been able to find the recipe for dinner."

"Yeah, I found it while we were picking up the kitchen."

She looked at all of us. "I will be back again in two hours, just before bedtime. I don't want to hear your music before I come into the house and I do NOT want to catch you on your mother's couch cushions again. Am I perfectly understood?"

"Yes, Sister Mason."

"Good. Enjoy your dinner and make sure your homework is done." And with one last stern glare about the room she left.

After she was gone we started working on dinner, after turning the music back on. Soon after eating we had gotten bored again and the couch cushions went back on the floor and the Lip-Synching Schofields began their crazy dance contest again. We did try to behave…for a while. But this time we kept an eye on the clock. When it reached time for her to come again to check on us, we made sure that the music was turned off, six children were in their pajamas, and the living room looked better than it had before our little adventure. She looked around. "Have you all finished your homework?"

"Yes."

"Have you all brushed your teeth?"

"Mine are clean, see?" John said proudly.

She smiled. "Well, then now it's time for bed. Jessica, your parents should be home within the next couple of hours. Make sure everyone is in bed before they get home, including you."

"Okay."

As far as I know, Sally never told my mom about our escapade. Then again, even if she did tell her, Mom probably wouldn't be all that surprised. She had some creative and, at times, foolhardy children.

Epilogue: Misadventure Continues…

As the years have passed, my siblings and I have found more opportunities for mischief and mayhem. Getting older hasn't really brought about growing up, just more creative ways of doing things. Though many of us are at the stage of being out of the house, we still get together often to recount the good times we had as children. John gets to participate in our fun from the stories we tell, since for most of our adventures he was either too small to remember them, or not yet born. We talk about the things we got away with and the ones we didn't. We remember the days of climbing trees, jumping out of windows, and burying treasure in the backyard. We remember the laughter, the fun and the wonder of childhood.

Now as I'm starting my own family I'm beginning to see that the Mother's Curse does in fact work. My walls are often colored on and my couch taken apart to become a castle. My son and daughter share a mischievous twinkle and I look with a mix of dread and excitement as to what their future will hold. Right now they're too little to get into too much trouble, but I know that the time will soon arrive that I will set three rules for my children:

1. Do not kill or permanently main each other.

2. When you make a mess clean it up.

3. Do NOT burn the house down.

Coming this holiday season:

Christmas Capers

The Schofield children are back in this heartwarming sequel to *Mischief, Mayhem, and NOT Burning the House Down*. Discover the joy and magic of the holidays as the Schofields learn what Christmas is really all about. Join them as they share their favorite memories of the season filled with fun, love and, of course, mischief.

The Schofield boys: John, Steven, and James

The Schofield girls: Jessica, Eliza and Bekah

Author Jessica L. Elliott grew up in Kansas with her five brothers and sisters. Together they embarked on many adventures, the most memorable being contained in this story. Despite there being a span of fifteen years between the oldest (Jessica) and the youngest (John), the six siblings are very close-knit, often being described by their mother as, "a box of puppies." These pictures were taken in March 2011 shortly before James left for Iceland, serving a two-year mission for the Church of Jesus Christ of Latter-day Saints.

For more information about Jessica L. Elliott and her books, visit www.JessicaLElliott.com or join her Facebook fanpage at www.facebook.com/JessicaLElliottAuthor.